CARS

This I-SPY book belongs to: _____

Introduction

I-Spy Cars covers a cross-section of the cars to be seen on European roads, from popular mass-production models to high-performance supercars, off-roaders to people carriers or MPVs from nostalgic to hybrid powered cars. More than 150 are illustrated, carefully chosen to be representative.

Some cars could not be included because of space. And, of course, manufacturers introduce new models throughout the year - some will undoubtedly appear while you are still spotting those in our selection. Remember too, that manufacturers often produce 'special editions' to entice customers, but these usually involve no more than trim and accessory enhancements and a good I-Spyer can usually recognize the car. Model names, even make names, can also be changed - General Motors' European models carrying Vauxhall or Opel badges are one example, another is the Mitsubishi Shogun, which is named Pajero in most countries.

Throughout we have selected photographs that will help you identify cars, then for each we give an impression of the model range - the variety of bodies and engines that have been listed - and often some idea of performance.

But do bear in mind that there are few roads in Europe where any of the cars in this book could legally be driven at their maximum speed! It is also important to remember the huge advances engineers have made in developing more fuel-efficient engines, and hybrid-engines that can switch between conventional and electric power. Body designs with a low 'drag-factor' help to reduce fuel consumption as do advanced tyre designs, which also play a vital role in the most important feature of all - safety.

The points score with each photograph is for the model family, not for the specific car illustrated. If you are an enthusiast you may like to I-Spy different types in a range, scoring 1 extra point for each variant.

Some car terms are explained on page 62 to help you understand the descriptions.

How to use your I-SPY book

Generally, cars appear in alphabetical order throughout the book, so it is easy to find a model. There are some minor changes to bring similar cars together while Land Rovers and Minis do not appear with their parent company's models. You need 1000 points to send off for your I-Spy certificate (see page 64) but that is not too difficult because there are masses of points in every book. As you make each I-Spy, write your score in the box.

I-SPY TITLES AVAILABLE:

Alfa Romeo is one of the most famous names in Italian motor cars and was founded in 1910. The name ALFA was created from the name Anonima Lombarda Fabbrica Automobili. The company was managed by Nicola Romeo and in 1920 the name was changed to Alfa Romeo with the Torpedo 20-30 Hp becoming the first car to be badged with the new company name. In 1923 a young racing driver named Enzo Ferrari joined Alfa Romeo and would later run their racing team before leaving to design and manufacture cars under his own name. Both brands are now under the ownership of Fiat. Often referred to as Alfa, they have a rich history in motor racing throughout the first part of the last century and have had victories in many races. Do you notice how many Alfas are in red, which is a favourite colour of Italians for cars?

MiTo

I-SPY points: 10

Date: _____

159

I-SPY points: 10

Date: _____

3

GT
I-SPY points: 10
Date: _____

BRERA
I-SPY points: 10
Date: _____

SPIDER
I-SPY points: 15
Date: _____

Audi can trace its origin back to 1899 but became a major car producer when four German car makers, Audi, Horch, DKW and Wanderer merged to form Auto Union in 1932. Now part of the Volkswagen Group along with other makes like Bentley, VW, Seat and Skoda, Audi is seen as an upmarket and prestige brand. Audi have enhanced their reputation for quality in recent years and now challenge the other top car makers for market share. Like many manufacturers, Audi takes part in motor races with much success to advertise their brand and recently became the first company to win the Le Mans 24 hour race with a diesel powered car. Most of Audi's range start with the letter A and then a number. The higher the number, the bigger and more expensive the car. Look out for Audi's distinctive TT model which now has a choice of diesel or petrol engines, which is unusual in a sports performance car. Take a special look at the Audi badge, with the four interlocking rings representing the four companies that merged to form Auto Union.

A3

I-SPY points: 5

Date: _____

A4

I-SPY points: 5

Date: _____

A5

I-SPY points: 5

Date: _____

A8

I-SPY points: 10

Date: _____

TT

score double points if you find a
diesel version.

I-SPY points: 10

Date: _____

6

BMW, Bayerische Motoren Werke (Bavarian Motor Works) was founded in 1916 primarily as a motorcycle and engine manufacturing company. After successfully making aircraft engines and motorcycles, BMW moved into car manufacturing but has had a remarkable transformation since the 1960s when it began to make high quality, executive cars. Since then BMW has established itself as maker of luxury cars. Unlike the 'older' manufacturers of cars, BMW is now involved in many racing activities, including Formula One to enhance their reputation. Today BMW focus on the high-end expensive car and motorcycle market and has the famous British names of Rolls Royce and Mini within its group. Take a special look at the BMW badge which is based upon a spinning propeller, representing their origins in aircraft engines.

1-SERIES

I-SPY points: 5

Date: _____

3-SERIES

I-SPY points: 5

Date: _____

I-SPY BMW

5-SERIES

I-SPY points: 5

Date: _____

I-SPY points: 15 for each model

Date: _____

X3, X5, X6

Score double points if you see an X6. These are new and are not so easy to find.

Z4

I-SPY points: 15

Date: _____

M-SERIES

Score double points if you find
an M series in the folding top
cabriolet 3 series model.

I-SPY points: 15

Date: _____

Chevrolet is one of the most iconic of American cars and is often referred to as Chevy. Started in 1911, Chevrolet became part of General Motors in 1917. Louis Chevrolet, the co-founder of the company was originally a racing driver hired by the Buick Motor Company in promotional races. General Motors positioned Chevrolet to sell in direct competition to Ford's famous Model T in the 1930s and is GM's largest selling brand, making all types of cars from small compacts to large saloon models. Most of Chevrolet's US models are not imported into the UK, and you are most likely to see the small compacts that started life under the name of Daewoo. This brand disappeared in 2003 and since then its ranges have carried the Chevrolet name. The most famous Chevys are the Corvette and the Camero sports cars, and if you are lucky you may see one on the roads in the UK. If you do find one, look where the driver sits. He will be on the 'wrong' side of the car as these cars are not made in right hand drive for British roads.

TACUMA
I-SPY points: 10

Date: _____

MATIZ
I-SPY points: 5

Date: _____

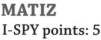

CRUZE
I-SPY points: 5

Date: _____

Founded by Andre Citroën in 1919, Citroën was the first mass production car manufacturer outside the USA. In 1934 Citroën produced the first mass produced front wheel drive car called the Traction Avant. Citroën are a famous French car maker that has had many technical innovations in their cars including special suspension on their cars in the 1950s and 60s using air to cushion the ride for the passengers. They are also famous for a car called the 2CV, which meant two horse power (engine power was originally measured as a reference to the number of horses that would be need to produce the same speed. The more horsepower, the more speed the engine could produce). This was a very simple car that was sold inexpensively in many countries of the world and was produced from 1948 through to 1990. In 1934, due to financial problems partly caused by the development costs of front wheel drive, Citroën was forced into foreclosure and was taken over by the Michelin Tyre Company. Since 1976 Citroën has been part of PSA Group, Peugeot Citroën Automobiles based in Paris.

C2

I-SPY points: 5

Date:

C1

I-SPY points: 5

Date:

PICASSO

I-SPY points: 5

Date:

Fiat is a very large manufacturer of all kinds of vehicles including cars and trucks. Based in Italy, they make a wide range of cars from small to large and also own Alfa Romeo and the very famous car maker Ferrari, who has a long history in motor racing, particularly Formula One. There is a very famous model called the Cinquecento or Fiat 500, a simple car with a small 500cc engine that was inexpensive to run and has become fashionable to own. Due to popularity, this car has recently been relaunched and is again very desirable. Look out for the striking colours on many of these.

500

Score double points if you find a white one with green and red stripes. These are the colours of the Italian flag.

I-SPY points: 10

Date: _____

PANDA
I-SPY points: 5

Date: _____

GRANDE PUNTO

I-SPY points: 10

Date: _____

BRAVO

I-SPY points: 5

Date: _____

The Ford Motor Company of America was started in 1903 and is one of the oldest car marques. It was one of the first manufacturers of mass produced cars in the world. Based in Detroit Michigan, which would later earn the nickname of 'Motor City', Ford went on to become one of the largest and most profitable companies in the world. Its founder, Henry Ford once famously said 'You can have any colour of car you like, as long as it's black'. This remark referred to the company's famous Model T, which was the first mass market car produced on an assembly line, a method that was to transform the manufacture of cars, making it easy, quick and less expensive as every car was basically the same. Henry Ford's vision changed car production forever and would be copied by all volume car makers over the world. Today Ford has factories worldwide and has been in continuous family control for over 100 years.

C-MAX

I-SPY points: 10

Date: _____

FIESTA

I-SPY points: 5

Date: _____

MONDEO
I-SPY points: 5

Date: _____

FUSION
I-SPY points: 10

Date: _____

KA
I-SPY points: 5

Date: _____

FOCUS
I-SPY points: 5

Date: _____

Honda of Japan started life as motorcycle makers and has sold and still sells, many millions of motorcycles all over the world. In the 1960s they started to make small engined motor cars, at first using similar engines to their motorcycles. Their first car had chain driven rear wheels using almost the same technology used in motorcycles. Honda is relatively new as a manufacturer, only starting after the World War II and like others has demonstrated its products through racing both motorcycles and cars in competition, including Formula One. Honda was the first Japanese maker to launch a dedicated luxury brand in 1986, the Acura, to win sales in the US markets.

ACCORD

I-SPY points: 5

Date: _____

CIVIC

I-SPY points: 5

Date: _____

CR-V

I-SPY points: 5

<u>Date:</u>

JAZZ

I-SPY points: 10

<u>Date:</u>

Hyundai are the fourth largest car maker in the world. This South Korean company started life in the construction business in 1947 and became South Korea's largest industrial company, with diverse businesses in many different industries including shipbuilding. The Hyundai Motor Company's first global success came from their Pony model that was particularly successful in the USA in the 1980s during the oil crisis, as it was far more economical than any of the American cars of the day.

SANTA FE

I-SPY points: 10

Date: _____

i10 & i20

I-SPY i10 points: 10

Date: _____

I-SPY i20 points: 10

Date: _____

Jaguar is a famous British marque and has a long history in making very fast sports and saloon cars, two-seaters as well as four-seaters. One of their most famous cars was the E-type two-seater sports car in the 1960s and early 70s. This car has a unique look and is very distinctive. Jaguar has had many victories in motor races over the years and is very proud of its success in the Le Mans 24 hour race in France, which is run through a full day and night. Many manufacturers like to take part in endurance events to show the reliability of their cars as they are at their maximum top speed for the whole race.

XK
I-SPY points: 15

Date: _____

XJ
I-SPY points: 15

Date: _____

X-TYPE
I-SPY points: 10

Date: _____

Jeep is a very famous 4x4 vehicle that has had a big part to play in both peace and wartime, during the last century and was the vehicle chosen by the US Army to move quickly over different types of terrain. From their early days of just making military type vehicles, Jeep has used its reputation of strength and reliability to make more refined off-road cars, mainly for the USA market. Today Jeep is part of the Chrysler Corporation.

COMPASS

I-SPY points: 10

Date:

PATRIOT

I-SPY points: 10

Date:

CHEROKEE

I-SPY points: 10

Date:

Kia Motors is South Korea's second largest car maker behind Hyundai. Founded in 1944 as a manufacturer of steel tubing and bicycles, Kia later went on to build motorcycles, trucks and cars. During the Asian financial crisis of 1997 Kia was sold to its rival Hyundai who have since sold part of the company but still remain involved in the business. In the past Kia have helped Mazda and Ford develop and produce cars for the local markets and this is a perfect example of how manufacturers who normally compete as rivals, cooperate with each other in order to enter certain markets and reduce their costs.

RIO

I-SPY points: 5

Date: _____

CEE'D

I-SPY points: 5

Date: _____

SOUL

I-SPY points: 5

Date: _____

Land Rover is probably the most famous off-road vehicle in the world. This British manufacturer has developed all kinds of vehicles, from a very basic model used by farmers that have changed little over the years, to larger luxury vehicles that can go both on and off-road. Look out for many older Land Rovers that can be seen, particularly in the countryside, as they have a reputation for reliability second to none.

DISCOVERY III
I-SPY points: 10

Date: _____

RANGE ROVER
I-SPY points: 10

Date: _____

FREELANDER
I-SPY points: 10

Date: _____

Lexus is the luxury brand of Toyota, and makes expensive luxury cars to compete with the other high-end companies like Mercedes, BMW and Audi. Lexus is a good example of a major manufacturer creating a new brand to compete in another section of the market that they would not normally be able to enter. Lexus do not make that many models but in a relatively short time have achieved a reputation for quality.

LS

I-SPY points: 10

Date: _____

GS

I-SPY points: 10

Date: _____

IS

I-SPY points: 10

Date: _____

SC

I-SPY points: 25

Date: _____

RX

I-SPY points: 15

Date: _____

This car maker is based in Hiroshima, Japan. Mazda is famous for using the Wankel Rotary engine in its vehicles, first introduced in 1967 as a way of making itself different from its rivals. Other car makers gave up on this design and Mazda are to date the only car manufacturer to persevere with the concept. Due to rising fuel costs, Mazda now only use their rotary engines in certain cars where they can utilise the power to weight advantage and all other cars in their model range use conventional piston engines. Since the 1960s Ford has been involved with Mazda and has worked on several projects with them and now owns part of the Mazda Car Company.

MAZDA3 MPS

I-SPY points: 10

Date: _____

MAZDA2

I-SPY points: 10

Date: _____

MAZDA6

I-SPY points: 10

Date: _____

RX-8

Score double points if you spotted that the rear doors have no handles and open the 'wrong' way. They are hinged at the rear of the door.

I-SPY points: 15

Date: _____

MX-5

Score double points if you spot an MX5 with a retractable metal roof. Unusually this car is available with either the normal soft top folding roof, or a metal retractable one.

I-SPY points: 15

Date: _____

Mercedes-Benz is one of the most prestigious car makers in the world. More commonly referred to as Mercedes, they are often the choice for the official cars of governments around the world and build special vehicles with many security benefits. Based in Stuttgart Germany, their badge, the three pointed star is recognised all around the world. They have often proven their cars in all types of racing over many years and are still involved in supplying engines to many Formula One teams. They make many different types of cars, from small four-door family cars, through to large executive saloons and two-seater sports cars.

A-CLASS
I-SPY points: 10

Date:

C-CLASS
I-SPY points: 10

Date:

E-CLASS
I-SPY points: 15

Date:

SLK

I-SPY points: 20

Date:_____

CLK

Score double points if you noticed that this car does not have a pillar between the front and rear windows. This gives the car a more sleek look, but is more difficult and expensive to make as the rest of the car has to be reinforced to keep its strength.

I-SPY points: 15

Date:_____

S-CLASS

I-SPY points: 15

Date:_____

The BMC Mini was made in 1959 in Birmingham by the British Motor Corporation and was an instant hit. At the time it was revolutionary, adopting a new front wheel drive engine and gearbox which was mounted transversally across the car enabling the car to be made smaller (hence the name) and as it was easier to assemble it was less expensive to make. The Mini has become iconic over the years and although now owned by Germany's BMW it is still made in Britain. Look out for the often very funky colourful designs that customise the Mini, many of which incorporate the Union Flag. The Mini has become a symbol of the British car industry and is recognised all over the world.

MINI

Score double points if you see a Mini decorated with the Union Flag.

I-SPY points: 20

Date: _____

MINI (BMW)

I-SPY points: 10

Date: _____

MINI CLUBMAN

I-SPY points: 15

Date: _____

Mitsubishi

The Mitsubishi Company was founded in1870 as a shipping firm, and has since become involved in many other industries, including coal mining, shipbuilding, banking and insurance. Car manufacture is just one side of this huge corporation. The Mitsubishi Corporation is Japan's largest trading company. In 1970 the car company was formed from the automotive division of Mitsubishi Heavy Industries. Chrysler, the US car maker has had an interest in this company almost from the time the car company was formed and joint ventures with Hyundai of South Korea and Proton of Malaysia again illustrate the cooperation between car makers in this global industry.

OUTLANDER

I-SPY points: 10

Date: _____

COLT

I-SPY points: 5

Date: _____

LANCER

I-SPY points: 5

Date: _____

Nissan

Nissan formerly sold cars under the Datsun name and was one of the first Japanese makers to sell cars in any volume in the UK with their small car, called the Datsun Cherry. Very quickly they established a good name in quality and value for money. Now sold worldwide under the Nissan name they are one of the major global manufacturers and have a close alliance with the French car manufacturer, Renault. In America they have established the Infiniti marque as an upper market brand to compete in the more expensive luxury sector and are now bringing these cars to Europe. Look for the new Infiniti models on the UK roads in the future.

MICRA

I-SPY points: 10

Date: _____

NOTE

I-SPY points: 10

Date: _____

QASHQAI

I-SPY points: 15

Date:

350Z

I-SPY points: 15

Date:

Peugeot's roots go back to a family business that was founded in 1810. In the early days the business was based around coffee milling and bicycle manufacturing in Sochaux in North East France. In 1858 the Peugeot family filed its trademark lion and in 1891 produced its first automobile. In 1896 Armand Peugeot founded the Société des Automobiles Peugeot. Today Peugeot is one of the three main French manufacturers, who along with Citroen share many ventures and design innovations. Peugeot have a particular reputation in designing efficient diesel engines and have an excellent history in off-road rallying, including the famous Monte Carlo Rally. In 1976 Peugeot and Citroen merged into one company to form PSA Peugeot Citroen based in Paris.

107

I-SPY points: 5

Date:

207

I-SPY points: 5

Date:

308
I-SPY points: 5

Date: _____

407
I-SPY points: 5

Date: _____

Porsche was founded in 1930 by Ferdinand Porsche and initially did not manufacture cars but was a consulting firm offering help to companies developing motor vehicles. One of the first tasks it undertook was on behalf of the German government to help develop a 'people's car' (in German volks wagen) which resulted in the formation of the Volkswagen (VW) company and launch of their Beetle car. The first model under the Porsche name was the Porsche 64 produced in 1939 and used many of the same components as the VW Beetle. Their most famous car, their 911 model was first produced in 1964 and the latest version has almost the same shape. The 911 is the model on which Porsche have built their reputation and have used it in many endurance races including the classic Le Mans 24 hour race in France in which they have competed over many years. Most Porsche cars are two-seater sports cars but they have recently made a four-seater car and a Sports Utility Vehicle (SUV) called the Cayenne.

BOXSTER
I-SPY points: 20

Date: _____

CAYMAN
I-SPY points: 25

Date: _____

CAYENNE

I-SPY points: 25

Date: _____

911

I-SPY points: 25

Date: _____

The Renault brothers (Louis, Marcel and Fernand) together with two of their friends began producing cars in 1897 and sold their first Voiturette 1 CV (meaning one horsepower) in 1898. Two years later the Renault Corporation was founded as 'Societe Renault Freres'. As well as cars, Renault also manufactured taxis, buses and trucks and during World War I (1914–18) made military equipment, including aeroplanes. Like the other two French car makers, Peugeot and Citroën, Renault has a long history in European motor manufacture. They have been prominent in motor racing across Europe at the very highest levels, including Formula One. The Renault Formula One team, in the mid 1970s, was the first ever team to race on radial tyres, an innovation pioneered by Michelin.

TWINGO

I-SPY points: 10

Date: _____

CLIO

I-SPY points: 5

Date: _____

MÉGANE
I-SPY points: 5

Date: _____

LAGUNA
I-SPY points: 5

Date: _____

SCENIC
I-SPY points: 10

Date: _____

The Rover name was amalgamated, along with other well known British names: Triumph, MG, Austin and Morris into the group known for some time as British Leyland. They were one of the main volume producers of motor vehicles in the UK along with Ford and Vauxhall (General Motors). The name Rover was adopted by the group in the late 1980s to give the cars a more up-market image as Rover was seen originally as a top end luxury car in Europe. Since then the Group has been split up and some of the brands sold to other manufacturers, including the Mini which is now owned by BMW.

25

I-SPY points: 5

Date: _____

75

I-SPY points: 5

Date: _____

45

I-SPY points: 5

Date: _____

Saab is a Swedish car maker that has a history in entering its cars in off-road rallying, a special type of motor sport on unmade roads and through forests. Like other makers, they wanted to demonstrate the reliability of their cars in very demanding conditions. Saab have a reputation for making strong cars and up until recently only made petrol engined cars due to the very cold conditions encountered particularly in its home country (diesel fuel can freeze at very low temperatures). Like some others, Saab has a history in making aircraft, including military planes and trucks. The truck division, Scania, is now owned by Volkswagen Group.

9-3

I-SPY points: 10

Date: _____

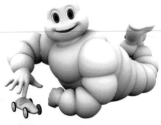

9-5

I-SPY points: 10

Date: _____

The name SEAT stands for Sociedad Española de Automóviles de Turismo and was founded in Spain in 1950 initially with assistance from Group Fiat. The SEAT 600, based on the Fiat 600 was the first mass produced car to be owned by many Spanish families. The collaboration with Fiat ended in 1981 and after producing cars independently, Audi/VW began a partnership in 1986, which resulted in the integration of SEAT into the Volkswagen Group. Their wide range of models and powerful performance engines has led to many more SEAT cars now seen on British roads.

IBIZA
I-SPY points: 10

Date: _____

LEÓN
I-SPY points: 5

Date: _____

ALTEA
I-SPY points: 10

Date: _____

Škoda

Škoda is a car manufacturer based in the Czech Republic and became a subsidiary of the Volkswagen Group in 1991. The origins of Škoda go back to the mid 1890s where the company started out manufacturing bicycles, when Václav Klement and Václav Laurin began their business. In 1899 their first motorcycle appeared and by 1905 the first car was produced. In 1924, after running into difficulties they sought a partner and merged with Škoda Works, the biggest industrial enterprise in Czechoslovakia at the time and adopted their name. They previously made inexpensive 'no frills' cars, but since the VW Group has taken them over they have enhanced their reputation and now appeal to many more customers. Škoda, like many others, could be seen in off-road rallying over the years and are still entered today.

FABIA
I-SPY points: 10

Date:

OCTAVIA
I-SPY points: 10

Date:

SUPERB
I-SPY points: 10

Date:

Smart are part of Mercedes Benz and are very distinctive in their design. Orignally they were just two-seater cars with economical three cylinder Mercedes engines and completely different from the other Mercedes models. Almost a reverse of Toyota's strategy when they created the Lexus luxury brand to enter the prestige market, Mercedes created with Smart a new type of small car that had not existed before. This type of car is particularly suited to those living and travelling in cities as it is very short in length and can be parked very easily.

FOURTWO

I-SPY points: 20

Date:

FORFOUR

I-SPY points: 20

Date:

ROADSTER

I-SPY points: 20

Date:

Subaru is a Japanese maker who first entered the UK market selling cars to those, including farmers and people living in remote parts of the country, who sometimes need to drive in difficult off-road places. This was due to all their cars having four-wheel drive where all the four wheels are driven by the engine. Normally cars are driven by two wheels, either the more traditional rear wheels, or increasingly more popular (as it makes manufacture easier and less expensive), the front wheels. Subaru's four-wheel drive cars make it able to access more difficult terrain and they have used this to their advantage in rallying where much of the race is off-road. Four-wheel drive is the choice of most manufacturers for their larger SUV's designed to go off-road, but Subaru are one of the few makers to adopt this design for all their cars.

FORESTER
I-SPY points: 15
Date: _____

LEGACY
I-SPY points: 10
Date: _____

IMPREZA

I-SPY points: 5

Date:

TRIBECA

I-SPY points: 10

Date:

Suzuki started life in 1909 by making weaving looms for the Japanese silk industry. Whereas most manufacturers began making motorcycles and then cars, unusually Suzuki started by making motor cars in 1937, but after the end of World War II started developing small motorcycles as the demand for cheap affordable transport in Japan grew. By 1952 Suzuki Motors was born. It is unusual for a motor company to start in cars, go on to motorcycles, and then back to cars. Today Suzuki is the 9th largest car maker in the world and one of the leading global motorcycle makers.

SWIFT
I-SPY points: 5
Date: _____

SPLASH
I-SPY points: 5
Date: _____

ALTO
I-SPY points: 5
Date: _____

Toyota is the largest motor car company in the world and has the luxury make Lexus in its family. In 1934 Toyota designed and built its first engine, followed in 1936 with the building of its first car. In 1937 the Toyota Motor Corporation was formed. Toyota was another company to profit from the oil crisis in the US and sales of their economical smaller cars which offered large fuel savings over the American cars of the day. This enabled Toyota to establish itself in the most lucrative of car markets, the USA. This early success allowed Toyota to set up factories in America making cars designed specifically for the US domestic markets and also build car plants in many other countries, including Britain. This growth as enabled Toyota to overtake General Motors as the largest car manufacturer in the world.

AVENSIS

I-SPY points: 5

Date: _____

RAV4

I-SPY points: 10

Date: _____

iQ
I-SPY points: 5

Date: _____

YARIS
I-SPY points: 10

Date: _____

Part of the big General Motors company, also referred to as GM, Vauxhall is the brand chosen for the UK. This is due to the reputation that Vauxhall has earned over the years. You may see a car with a foreign number plate in the UK that looks just like a Vauxhall. It will most likely carry the Opel badge, as that is the brand GM uses in all other European countries. These models are very similar and could even be made in the same factories. There are many types of Vauxhall cars ranging from small cars to large four-seater saloons but Vauxhall's strength is mainly found in the mid-range cars supplied to companies and 'big fleet' users.

CORSA

I-SPY points: 5

Date:

ASTRA

I-SPY points: 5

Date:

ZAFIRA

I-SPY points: 10

Date: _____

INSIGNIA

I-SPY points: 5

Date: _____

VECTRA

I-SPY points: 5

Date: _____

The literal translation of this German name is 'Peoples Car' and the company was originally started to provide the people of Germany with an inexpensive affordable car in the 1930s. This car was called the Beetle due to its shape and became a huge success. It was unusual in that it had the engine mounted in the rear of the car and to keep the design simple the engine was cooled by the air flowing around it. This car, in almost its original design remained in production for nearly 50 years and like the Mini and the Fiat 500 has recently been relaunched due to the appeal of the shape and the ongoing demand from customers. The new Beetle, whilst having a very similar shape to the original, has a water cooled engine mounted in the front driving the front wheels. More recently, VW's Golf model, has enjoyed similar success to the iconic Beetle, having undergone many changes since its introduction in 1974. This maker is more likely to be called by its shortened name of VW, and has an impressive number of manufacturers in the group, such as Bentley, Bugatti, Lamborghini, Audi, Seat and Skoda as well the Volkswagen brand itself.

BEETLE - OLD

I-SPY points: 25

Date: _____

BEETLE - NEW

I-SPY points: 15

Date: _____

POLO

I-SPY points: 5

Date:_____

PASSAT

I-SPY points: 5

Date:_____

GOLF

I-SPY points: 5

Date:_____

SHARAN

I-SPY points: 10

Date:_____

Volvo is a Swedish car maker which has established a reputation for making cars with very high safety features. They are seen as a quality manufacturer and now have many models of car including cabriolets (whose roof folds down and are very popular in the summer). This is a fairly recent development and shows how the company has changed since it was bought by the Ford Motor Company. Like Saab, Volvo were very late in offering diesel engines in their cars due to the very cold conditions in their home market. You will see many Volvo trucks on the roads that were originally part of the same company but are now independent following the sale of the car division to Ford.

XC60, XC70, XC90

I-SPY points: 10

Date: _____

V50, V70

I-SPY points: 5

Date: _____

S40, S80
I-SPY points: 5

Date: _____

C30, C70
Score double points if you see a C70 with a retractable folding metal roof. Great in the summer for all four passengers!

I-SPY points: 5

Date: _____

FERRARI

Classic Italian sports cars founded by Enzo Ferrari in 1928.

I-SPY points: 30

Date: _____

LOTUS

British sport car manufacturer since 1952. Current models include the Elise and the Exige.

I-SPY points: 20

Date: _____

LAMBORGHINI

Lamborghini produce some of the most powerful and expensive sport cars seen on the roads.

I-SPY points: 30

Date: _____

TVR

British light-weight sport cars that use a straight-6 cylinder or V8 engine.

I-SPY points: 25

Date: _____

ASTON MARTIN

British car manufacture since 1913 and well-known for being James Bond's preferred choice of vehicle.

I-SPY points: 25

Date: _____

MASERATI

Italian sports car under Fiat ownership.

I-SPY points: 30

Date: _____

BENTLEY

Luxury executive cars now owned by VW. Often used by royalty and statesmen. Score double points if you see a white one. Often used as wedding cars. See if the bride and groom are in the back of the car!

I-SPY points: 25

Date: _____

ROLLS ROYCE

Famous for featuring its mascot "The Spirit of Ecstasy" at the front of the car. Now owned by BMW. Score double points if you see a white one.

I-SPY points: 20

Date: _____

I-SPY points: 15
Double for a pink one

Date: _____

LIMOUSINE

Mostly driven by chauffeurs as transport to parties and weddings. Many come with televisions, video players and bars as standard.

RELIANT ROBIN

Introduced to the UK in 1973, score double points if you see a yellow van version. Look to see if Del and Rodney from 'Only Fools and Horses' are in it!

I-SPY points: 15

Date: _____

CITROËN 2CV

If you are really lucky, you may see the 2CV in a van version. Double points if you do. If you do the colour will probably be grey! Most of them were as this is a neutral 'working' colour.

I-SPY points: 20

Date: _____

I-SPY points: 20

Date: _____

VW CAMPER VAN

The VW Camper Van was first produced in 1950 and became very popular in the 1960s as a 'hippie van', often with hand-painted designs and a peace sign as replacement for the Volkswagen logo.

58

MORRIS MINOR

A classic British car dating from 1948. Score double points points if you see a 'Traveller' version, the estate model. Note the use of wood on the rear part of the car, inspired by the American cars in the 1950s.

I-SPY points: 25

Date: _____

HILLMAN IMP

In production from 1963-1976, the Hillman Imp was a saloon car with the engine at the rear made to rival the Mini.

I-SPY points: 15

Date: _____

G-WIZ

The G-Wiz is the best-selling electric car to date. Produced in India, the car is a small city hatchback classified as a 'heavy quadricycle' (quad bike) which makes it exempt from city congestion charges.

I-SPY points: 20

Date: _____

AIXAM MEGA

Small French microcar classed as a "quad bike' hence you only need a motorcycle licence to drive one. Not noted for speed, but ideally suited for inner-city driving.

I-SPY points: 25

Date: _____

MYCAR

Italian styled electric car and winner of the 2008 Electric Car of the Year award. With its zero CO_2 emission it qualifies for free road tax and can be charged from any domestic electric socket.

I-SPY points: 25

Date: _____

TOYOTA PRIUS HYBRID

Winner of the Car of the Year 2005 award, the Prius was the first mass-produced hybrid car. As a hybrid the car uses a petrol engine and electric motor. The car switches to electric mode at low speeds.

I-SPY points: 15

Date: _____

HONDA CIVIC HYBRID

A saloon car which like the Toyota Prius uses hybrid technology. The car runs on petrol and charges the electric engine when braking or coasting. This aids fuel economy and reduces CO_2 emissions.

I-SPY points: 15

Date: _____

LEXUS HYBRID (GS, LS, RX)

Lexus has three car models available with the hybrid technology. The GS Hybrid is a mid-sized saloon, the LS a large luxury saloon and the RX is a crossover SUV.

I-SPY points: 15

Date: _____

4WD
Four-wheel drive, meaning all four wheels receive power from the engine at the same time.

concept car
Car prototype made to showcase new features often presented at motor shows for public opinion. Some concepts may never be put into production.

convertible
A car with a retractable roof to make it open-air.

coupé
Usually a hard-topped two-seater with sporting characteristics.

crossover SUV
A car produced from a car platform but with SUV features.

estate
A saloon with larger boot space. Sometime described as a 'station wagon'

flagship
Term use to denote the top of the range car from a manufacturer.

front-wheel drive
Almost universal on small cars and some medium models, this layout has the engine and transmission at the front of the car, driving the front wheels

hatchback
Small car body style with a sloping, hinged rear door that opens upwards. Sometimes referred to as a 3- or 5-door.

hot hatch
High-performance hatchback.

hybrid
Car that runs on both petrol or diesel and electricity.

MPV
Multi-purpose Passenger Vehicle or people carrier.

roadster
An open car with sporting characteristics. Usually a convertible.

saloon
Car with two rows of seats with adequate space for adults in the back.

supercar
Very high-performance cars. Usually expensive to buy and run and seldom practical for everyday use.

supermini
Car which is classed larger than a city car, but smaller than a small family car

SUV
Sport Utility Vehicle often with off-road capabilities.

Index

First published by Michelin Maps and Guides 2009
© Michelin, Proprietaires-Editeurs 2009.
Michelin and the Michelin Man are registered
Trademarks of Michelin.
Created and produced by Blue Sky Publishing Limited.
All rights reserved. No part of this publication may be
reproduced, copied or transmitted in any form without
the prior consent of the publisher.
Print services by FingerPrint International Book
production - fingerprint@pandora.be
The publisher gratefully acknowledges the contribution
of the I-Spy team; Camilla Lovell, Ruth Neilson, Ian
Black and Ian Murray in the production of this title.
The publishers are grateful for the kind assistance and
reproduction rights granted by all the manufacturers and
agencies illustrated within this I-Spy book.
Thanks also to Unitaw Limited and Great Escape
Classic Car Hire for supplying photographs in this book.
Other images in the public domain and used under a
creative commons license. All logos, images designs
and image rights are © the copyright holders and are
used with thanks and kind permission.
Reprinted 2010   10 9 8 7 6 5 4

I-SPY
One Token
715137

HOW TO GET YOUR I-SPY CERTIFICATE AND BADGE

Every time you score 1000 points or more in an I-Spy book, you can apply for a certificate

Here's what to do, step by step:

Certificate

- Ask an adult to check your score
- Ask his or her permission to apply for a certificate
- Apply online to www.ispymichelin.com
- Enter your name and address and the completed title
- We will send you back via e mail your certificate for the title

Badge

- Each I-Spy title has a cut out (page corner) token at the back of the book
- Collect five tokens from different I-Spy titles
- Put Second Class Stamps on two strong envelopes
- Write your own address on one envelope and put a £1 coin inside it (for protection). Fold, but do not seal the envelope, and place it inside the second envelope
- Write the following address on the second envelope, seal it carefully and post to:

I-Spy Books
Michelin Maps and Guides
Hannay House
39 Clarendon Road
Watford
WD17 1JA